TEMPLES OF CONVENIENCE

LUCI...

GORDON FRASER

LONDON 1978

First published 1978 by
The Gordon Fraser Gallery Ltd., London and Bedford
Text and photographs copyright © Lucinda Lambton 1978
ISBN 0 86092 010 0

696. 182.

Lambton, Lucinda
  Temples of convenience
  1. Privies—Pictorial Works
  I. Title
  696'. 182   TD775
  ISBN 0-86092-010-0

201885400.

Made and printed in Great Britain by
Westerham Press, Westerham, Kent
Designed by Peter Guy

TO PAUL KEEGAN

ACKNOWLEDGEMENTS

I would like to thank all the following people for their kindness, which was often carried to astonishing lengths. It manifested itself in all manner of ways; patience, helpfulness, generosity, hospitality etc, and I am extremely grateful to each and every person mentioned.

Roger Acking, for letting me have his lavatory seat for three weeks. Mr Frank Alflatt of the Science Museum for consistent kindness and cheerfulness, Mr Lesley Andrews, Mrs Daphne Archibald, Mr M.Y. Ashcroft M.A. County Archivist of North Yorkshire, John Aspinall, Lord Barnard, Mr and Mrs Jeremy Barr. Francesca Barran of the National Trust for helping time and time again with various problems. Mr and Mrs V.T. Berry, The Misses Matilda and Betty Besso who allowed their bathroom to be photographed for seven hours. John and Prudence Binning, Mrs Ruby Bloud, Mr S.R. Bostel grandson of the first producer of the wash-out closet who went to an enormous amount of trouble over the course of a year to gather every scrap of information that he could for the book. Alison Britton whose beautifully designed tiles were sadly not finally included. Mr R.T. Buck of Dent and Hellyer Ltd, The Marquis of Bute for repeated and generous hospitality. Mrs Walter Caley, Mr Thomas Caunce, Ian Chadwell for hours and hours of his time, John Chesshyre, Dr J.A. Coiley of the National Railway Museum at York, Mrs Robin Compton, Martin Cooke, The Lady Diana Cooper, Nicholas Cooper, Bobby Corbett, Dan Cruickshank for years of kindness and patience, Mr and the late Mrs Cotrell-Dormer. Geoff Dale of Doulton Sanitaryware Ltd., Warren Davis of the National Trust, Mr Ernest Delaney, The Duchess of Devonshire, John Dinkle Keeper of Brighton Pavilion and his wife Camilla. Mr and Mrs Anthony Drewe, Martin Drury of the National Trust, Mr J. Edwards of the Victoria and Albert Museum, Valerie Elliot, Stanley Ellis of Twyfords Ltd, Christopher Gibbs, Jim Gibson of Twyfords whose cheerfulness and help over a year was remarkable. Arthur Grogan, Wendy Gutteridge who wrote the book out twice in longhand. Robin Haddow who held at least fifty Ibrox Park football fans at bay from the stained glass gents in the Old Toll Bar Glasgow, as well as inumerable other kindnesses. Miss Hallam, Henry Harrod, my two boys Barnaby and Huckleberry Harrod, Peter and Gay Hartley, Cyril Hayson, Miles Hildyard and Mrs Sybil Hildyard, Sally Holden of the North Cornwall Museum and Gallery, Mr Holland, Mr and Mrs David Hudson, Miss Ilbert, Paul Keegan for his hours of valuable research, Mrs Issac, Katya Krausova, Mrs Elaine Lanchester Librarian of West Dean College, The Marquis and Marchioness of Londonderry, Miss Frances Lovering of Doulton and Company, Jim Lowe, Angus McBean, Mr Murdo MacDonald District Archivist of the Argyll and Bute District Council, David McLaughlin, Mr Margrie, Tony Miles, David and Martha Mlinaric for wonderous friendship, David Moore, Mr J. Morris, Mr Geoffrey Moorehouse, Mr D.C. Muir, Mrs J.E. Nelmes, Bob and Phyl Parker of the National Trust, Patrick and Judith Phillips, Mr Geoffrey Pidgeon great grandson of the inventor of the wash-down closet. John and Rosalind Powell-Jones of the National Trust, Jiminy and Emily Read, Dr J.R. Reid, David Rhodes, Mr Ring of the Southport Cricket Club, John Ryan, The Hon Hugh Sackville-West. Mrs Salvin, Pauline Sargent of South Glamorgan County Council who was tireless in producing new information for the book. David Sekkers of the Gladstone Pottery Museum and his wife Simone, Houston Shaw-Stewart, Jeff Smith, Ian Smythe, Joan Stacey, The Rev Nicholas and the Hon Mrs Stacey, Elizabeth Steele, Chairman Stirling, Miss Magda Stirling, Mrs Susan Stirling. The Right Reverend The Lord Bishop of Southwell and Mrs Wakeling, Len Spiers, Mr Bertram Swainson of the National Trust, Dr Taylor, Emma and Toby Tennant, Clissold Tuely and Miles Tuely. Paul Tomasso, Mr E. Tomkins, Jack and Jane Tressider, Mr John Tustin of Doulton and Company, Mr J. Vallance of the Wigan College of Technology, Mr and Mrs Eric Walker, Mr Waugh of Armitage Shanks Ltd. Bron and Teresa Waugh, The Duke of Wellington, Lieutenant Commander P.C. Whitlock of H.M.S. Victory, Mr H.G. White, Tony Whitmore, Mrs Joan Wilson, Mr W.G. Wright, Mr and Mrs Gerald Yorke and John and Jeannie Yorke.

SELECT BIBLIOGRAPHY

Catalogues and Magazines

Catalogues issued by all the companies mentioned in the introduction were consulted as well as the following magazines: *The Builder*, 1845–1850; *The Builders Magazine of Designs in Architecture*, 1774; *Illustrated London News*, 17 August 1850 (new shower bath); *Industries of the South Coast*, 1891; *The Metropolitan*, 15 July 1882, 'Manufactures of Public Utility'; *The Plumber*, 1 April 1922; *The Sanitary Record*, 23 April 1897, 'A pioneer in Sanitary Engineering'; *Speculum*, July 1934, 'Latrines and Cess-pools of Mediaeval London'; *The Surveyor and Municipal and County Engineer*, 11 Jan 1894, 'A new underground convenience'.

Books

ALLEN, E. *Wash and Brush Up*. London: A. & C. Black, 1976.

ASHE, G. *The Tale of the Tub*. London: Newman Neame, 1950.

BARNARD, JULIAN. *Victorian Ceramic Tiles*. London: Studio Vista, 1972.

BECKMAN, JOHANN. *A History of Inventions and Discoveries*. Translated by W. Johnston. 4 vols. 1971.

BOURKE, CAPTAIN JOHN G. *Scatalogic Rites of All Nations*. Washington D.C.: W.H. Lowdermilk, 1891.

BRIGGS, ASA. *Victorian Cities*. London: Penguin, 1963.

CRUNDEN, JOHN. *Convenient and Ornamental Architecture beginning with the Farm House and regularly ascending to the Most Grand and Magnificent Villa*. London, 1767.

DONNO, E. S. *Sir John Harington's A New Discourse of a Stale Subject, called the Metamorphosis of Ajax*. London, 1962.

DE VRIES, L. *Victorian Inventions*. London: J. Murray, 1971.

DYOS AND WOLF. *The Victorian City*. London: Routledge, 1976.

EASSIE, W. *Sanitary Arrangements for Dwellings*. London, 1874.

EYLES, DESMOND. *Royal Doulton 1815–1965, The Rise and Expansion of the Royal Doulton Potteries*. London, 1965.

GARLAND, MADGE. 'The Town Houses of Halsey Ricards'. *Country Life*. 13 and 20 November 1975.

GIROUARD, MARK. *The Victorian Country House*. Oxford: Oxford University Press, 1971.

HARINGTON, SIR JOHN. *The Metamorphosis of Ajax*. 1596.

HELLYER, BERTRAM. *Under Eight Reigns*. Dent and Hellyer. London, 1930.

HELLYER, S. STEVENS. *The Plumber and Sanitary Houses*. London: Batsford, 1877.

HELLYER, S. STEVENS. *The Principles and Practices of Plumbing*. London: Bell, 1891.

LAMB, H.A.J. 'Sanitation: An Historical Survey'. *The Architects Journal*. 4 March 1937.

LOUDON, JOHN CLAUDIUS. *The Architectural Magazine and Journal of Improvement in Architecture Building and Furnishing and in the Various Arts and Trades connected therewith*. London: Longman, 1834.

LUCAS, C. *An Essay on Waters*. London, 1756.

MCNEIL, IAN. *Joseph Bramah*. Newton Abbot: David and Charles, 1968.

MAYHEW, HENRY. *Mayhew's London, Selections from 'London Labour and the London Poor'*. Ed. P. Quennell. London, 1949.

MIDDLETON, G.A.T. *The Drainage of Town and Country Houses*. London, 1903.

MOORE, E.C.S. *Sanitary Engineering. A Practical Treatise*. London, 1898.

NEWMAN, HAROLD. 'Bourdalous'. *The Connoisseur*. December 1970 and March 1971.

PALMER, ROY. *The Water Closet, A New History*. Newton Abbot: David and Charles, 1973.

POORE, DR GEORGE VIVIAN. *The Dwelling House*. London: Longman, 1897.

PUDNEY, JOHN. *The Smallest Room*. London: M. Joseph, 1954.

QUENNEL, MARJORIE AND C.B. *A History of Everyday Things in England*. London, 1933.

READ, CHARLES HANDLEY. 'Notes on William Burgess's Painted Furniture'. *Burlington Magazine*. 1963.

REYBURN, WALLACE. *Flushed with Pride, the Story of Thomas Crapper*. London: McDonald, 1969.

REYNOLDS, REGINALD. *Cleanliness and Godliness*. London: Allen and Unwin, 1943.

ROBINS, F.W. *The Story of Water Supply*. Oxford: Oxford University Press, 1946.

ROLLESTON, SAMUEL. *Philosophical Dialogue Concerning Decency, to which is added a Critical and Historical Dissertation on Places of Retirement for Necessary Occasions, together with an Account of the Vessels and Utensils in Use among the Ancients, being a Lecture read before a Society of Learned Antiquaries*. 1971.

ROUTH, JONATHAN. *The Good Loo Guide*.

SCOTT, G.R. *The Story of Baths and Bathing*. London: T. Werner Laurie, 1939.

TREVELYAN, GEORGE MACAULEY. *Illustrated Social History in Four Volumes*. London: Pelican, 1964.

WALPOLE, HORACE. *Selected Letters*. Ed. by M.A. Pink. Scholar's Library. London, 1938.

WALSH, JOHN HENRY. *A Manual of Domestic Economy suited to Families spending from £100 to £1000 a Year*. London, 1857.

WARE, ISAAC. *A Complete Body of Architecture*. London, 1735.

WEBSTER, THOMAS. *An Encyclopedia of Domestic Economy*. London: Longman, 1844.

WRIGHT, L. *Clean and Decent*. London: Routledge, 1960.

T HE FIRST LAVATORY WITH working parts and flushing water was invented by Sir John Harington, the godson of Queen Elizabeth I, in 1596. 'This devise of mine' wrote Harington in his *Metamorphosis of Ajax*, a learned and elaborate treatise on the water closet, 'requires not a sea full of water, but a cisterne, not a whole Tems (Thames) full, but halfe a tunne full, to keep all sweete and savourie.' He installed one in his house at Kelstone near Bath and one for his godmother, the Queen, at Richmond Palace, but all the enticing words were to no further avail. He was 179 years before his time. The reeking stinking years were to go on until 1775 when the first successful patent for a water closet was taken out, although James I had granted one in 1617, but nothing more was heard of it.

The Romans, of course, had established an extraordinarily sophisticated, elegant and efficient sanitary system in England. From the splendour of the baths at Bath (Aquae Sulis) to the dextrous construction of a most ordinary length of piping one finds an astonishing understanding and appreciation for sanitary needs that was not to appear again on such a scale for over one hundred and fifty years. The baths with pools of hot and cold water, with sweating rooms and showers – where you were rubbed with ointments, oil, and sand if especially dirty, then scraped clean with a metal 'strigil' – were sumptuously comfortable. All these baths were public so there was little need to have one in your own home.

Less appealingly, the latrines too were public. At Housteads on the Roman wall in Northumberland as many as twenty men could sit and enjoy the sight and company of their companions, sending their offerings to Stercutius and Crepitus, the gods of ordure and conveniences, and Cloacina, the goddess of the common sewer. The Victorians were to remember Cloacina with these delightful words:

Oh Cloacina Goddess of this place,
Look on thy servant with a smiling face
Soft and cohesive let my offering flow
Not rudely swift nor obstinantly slow.

The Romans painted their walls with deities and other hallowed emblems to protect them against 'such as commit nuisance' and announced 'the wrath of heaven against those who should be impious enough to pollute what it was their duty to reverence.' (*Vestiges of ancient manners and customs*, Reverend John James Blunt.) Vessels were put at street corners for relief, which were used without charge until Vespasian, seeing this valuable liquid flowing so freely, placed a tax on their use, letting them out at the same time to those who would profit from the urine – fullers of cloth. Pliny noticed that the Roman fullers who used human urine for their business never suffered from gout. (*Scatalogical rites.*)

There were no latrines or privies attached to the houses, basins and pots were used, brought and emptied by slaves employed exclusively for this purpose. 'When a gentleman wanted his chamber-pot, it was a common way of speaking to make a noise with the finger and thumb by snapping them together, this was called "concrepare digitos".' (Petronius.)

The most miserable fate awaited many who walked beneath the window at night when the contents of these pots were thrown down into the street drains below. 'Clattering the storm descends from heights unknown'. (Third Satire of Juvenal.) Dryden translated the grim possibilities further:

'T is want of sense to sup abroad too late
Unless thou first hast settled thy estate;
As many fates attend thy steps to meet
As there are waking windows in the street:
Bless the good gods and think thy chance is rare
To have a piss-pot only for thy share.

There was of course no lavatory paper in the public latrines, sponge sticks were kept in containers of salt water or dipped into running water and used by one and all. The poorer Roman might use a stone instead for cleansing or perhaps a shell or a bunch of herbs.

The luxuriant depravity of the Romans reached its peak with the chamber pots and other such vessels being made of rare stones and metals. 'It would have been well', wrote Rolleston in 1751, 'for the Romans if they had but remained contented with earthen jurdens – we may date the commencement of [their] ruin from the introduction of gold and silver chamber pots and close stool pans.'

The next person to emerge from the shadowy ages of sanitary history was Boniface, who wrote the first Latin grammar in England, when he spoke out against mixed bathing in 745. It was the social licentiousness of it that he was decrying rather than the social cleansing of the body, but to the early Christian Church washing had become a most viceful activity, and this cultivation of the body was a luxury that had to be denied. St. Francis of Assisi, considering water to be one of the most precious of 'sisters' denied himself of it and St. Catherine of Siena as well as never washing attempted an even more tortuous form of self denial from daily relief.

Confusingly and conversely, water was required for most holy baptismal and purifying rites and by the twelfth century religious houses were using it freely to establish their healthy and holy lives. Physical cleanliness became an image of spiritual cleanliness. A very early account exists of Ethelwold, Abbot of Abingdon, who is recorded as having made a water course (ductum aquae) in 960 which ran under the dormitory to the 'Hokke' stream. This was obviously an efficient diversion of a stream or a conveniently placed spring source, and is the first detailed post-Roman account of sanitation in England. The next and more elaborate development was that which was carried out between 1150 and 1175 in the Christ Church Monastery and the Cathedral Priory at Canterbury where a complete and complex drainage system was laid down with underground pipes, filtered settling tanks, cisterns, baths and constantly trickling lavers.

The monastery at Durham too had an elaborate water course with the magnificent addition of an immense laver 'a fair laver or conduit, for the monks to wash their hands and faces at, being made in form round and covered with lead, and all of marble, saving the very outermost walls.' (*The Ancient Rites of Durham*, quoted by Willis.)

The privies at Durham are also described in *The Ancient Rites :* 'there was a fair large house and a most decent place adjoining to the west side of the said dorter [dormitory] towards the water, for the monks and the novices to resort unto, called the privies, which was made of two great pillars of stone that did bear up the whole roof thereof, and every seat and partition was of wainscot close on either side very decent so that one of them could not see one another, when they were in that place.'

The holy orders set an example to all. At St. Albans Cathedral excavations of the Great Cloister were carried out in 1924 and according to H.A.J. Lamb, writing in the *Architects Journal* in 1937: 'Here was found a deep pit. . . . At the bottom were found pieces of pottery and fragments of coarse cloth which, it is thought, were old gowns torn up by the monks and used as toilet paper. Evidence, too, that the monks suffered from digestive troubles, which were by no means rare in those days, was proved by finding in the pit, seeds of the blackthorn – a powerful aperient.'

At Southampton in 1290 the Friars were given a licence to take the waters from the Caldwell Spring and in 1310 they allowed the town an offshoot from their supply. Many towns benefited from the religious houses in this way; in 1451 the Bishop of Wells agreed with the Burgesses to supply water to the city with a pipe from his conduit house and in return for this favour the Burgesses were to pray for the Bishop once a year. Whilst the Bishop in return granted them 40 days indulgences.

London received its first water supply in 1237 when King Henry III requested that a certain Gilbert de Sandford should grant to the city the springs and waters in his lands at Tyburn.

The first major sanitary act to be passed in London was in 1358, when the 'Chancellor of the University' was required by Royal writ 'to remove from the streets and lanes of the town all swine and all dirt, dung, filth . . . and to cause the streets and lanes to be kept clean for the future.' There had been an earlier act of 1189 'concerning the necessary chambers [cesspits] in the houses of citizens'. This act was an unhappy necessity as was shown in 1328, all too long after it should have been implemented, when a William Sprot complained to the Assize of his neighbours, two brothers William and Adam Mere who had filled their 'cloaca' to overflowing so that it had seeped through his wall. The pit had not been the required distance away. At an Assize Court in 1347 two men were accused of piping their 'ordure' into their neighbour's cellar, which villainous act had not been discovered until the cellar had begun to overflow.

Cesspits were an alternative to open drains, sewers and the turgid rivers into which they flowed. In 1355 the River Fleet for example was choked stiff with filth. It should have been deep enough to float a boat laden up with a ton of wine, but had been allowed to get into such an extreme state from the eleven overhanging latrines and the three sewers that disgorged into it that it had ceased to flow.

Public latrines in medieval Britain were mostly built over the rivers and would have been used by local people as their only convenience as well as by the daily business population. There were many communal latrines built for tenements though pots were again an unpleasant alternative with the contents simply being thrown out onto the streets and the passers-by below. The open drains were clogged with foul rubbish, putrid entrails 'swine dirt dung [and] filth'. It became so bad that the Common Council appointed 'scavengers' to clean the streets and imposed fines on those people who added to the dirt. Shakespeare's father was fined for both leaving refuse in the streets and for failing to keep his gutters clean (*Cleanliness and Godliness*) and the Rector of St. Botolphs had to appear before the Assize of Nuisances for having allowed offensive piles of filth to accumulate around his new privy. (*Building in England down to 1540*).

The privies and latrines, both public and private, had to be cleaned as well. A cesspit with the accumulated filth of months was an atrocious prospect for the 'rakers' or 'gongfermors', as they were called (*gong* from the Saxon *gang*, to go off and *fey* from the Saxon verb to cleanse) and their pay was handsome: some forty shillings (£2) a job. One such gong-fermor, known as Richard the Raker, met with a dreadful death in his own privy in 1326 when he fell through the rotten planks and drowned 'monstrously in his own excrement'. (*The Black Death*.) The tale of the 'Jew of Tewkesbury' in 1259 is equally grim: he fell into a privy pit one Saturday and out of respect for his Sabbath allowed no one to pull him out. On Sunday with the mysterious intervention of the Earl of Gloucester he was not allowed to be rescued and by Monday he was dead. (*Scatalogical Rites*.)

Writing of all this filth casts a misleading light on medieval sanitation, the Assize of Nuisance were continuously busy with cases of 'annoyance' which shows that efforts were being made. Westminster Palace was the first lay house to have an underground drainage system. Henry III ordered to be made 'a certain conduit through which the refuse of the Kings kitchens at Westminster Palace flows into the Thames. Which conduit the King ordered to be made on account of the stink of the dirty water which was carried through his halls, which was wont to effect the health of the people frequenting the same halls.' (*Liberate Roll 44*.) Henry III had privies, garderobes, wardrobes, privy chambers and necessary places built into all his houses. (*Domestic Architecture in the Middle Ages*.)

Privy is an early middle-English word which comes from the Latin *privatus* meaning apart, retired, secret, not publicly known. The word garderobe is sometimes confused with wardrobe: the wardrobe was the room adjoining the privy in which you might wash and dress, clothes were kept in it and sewing and dressmaking might also be done there. Garderobe was the term most generally used for the castle or grander domestic privy which would often be built into the thickness of a wall and approached by a right-angled passage, a kind of horizontal trap that tried to keep the odours from escaping. Otherwise garderobes could be corbelled or simply built out from the wall which placed the privy as far away as possible and allowed everything to fall freely in to the moat, the river, the stream, pit or the ground below.

Marlowe's Edward II was kept in the garderobe pit at Berkeley Castle whilst the Queen and the nobles decided on his fate ('This dungeon where they keep me is the Sink/wherein the filth of all the castle falls.'). King James I of Scotland and King Edmund Ironside were killed whilst actually in the privy, and Richard III, according to Sir John Harington in his *Metamorphosis of Ajax*, was 'sitting on the draught' when he devised with Tirril how to have his nephews privily murdered.

Sir John Harington wrote his *Metamorphosis*, which he entreated should not be considered 'a noysome and un-savoury discourse' in 1596. It was an entertaining diatribe against the filthy habits of his fellow men, habits which he felt he could solve by his invention of the water closet. Queen Elizabeth, who had a bath once a month 'whether she needed it or no' (*Clean and Decent*), kept a copy of the *Metamorphosis of Ajax* chained to the wall beside her water closet at Richmond Palace. Other than Harington's own and the Queen's, as far as is known, not another of his devices was made: James I, Charles I and II and James II were all to prefer close stools, exquisite little velvet chests in appearance, but far from exquisite in the way that they worked: they were simply sumptuously disguised pots. At least two still survive today, one is at Hampton Court, the other at Knole in Kent. Henry VIII had a magnificent close stool with the important and interesting addition of 'sesstornes' (cisterns). It was covered with black velvet, studded with two thousand gilt nails and decorated with ribbons and fringes. The seat and the 'elbows', whose addition makes it sound like the finest throne, were covered with white 'fuschan' and stuffed with down. Two leather cases were made, one for the pot and the cisterns, the other for the stool, which suggests that it was taken with the King on his travels. (*Connoisseur*.) In the inventory of Kenilworth the Earl of Leicester was shown to have owned twenty-eight close stools, sixteen of which were of black velvet or satin, both quilted and plain, and garnished with either lace or fringes of silver or gold.

Close stools were certainly more comfortable than their predecessors, the garderobes, but hardly more sanitary. Buckets and pots, sometimes with the added comfort of a cushion or a green baize seat, were the alternatives with the same old repulsive habit of their being emptied out onto the streets. One poor fellow, written of in the early 1600s, 'the Fool of Lincoln', who after his wife had 'so reviled him with tongue nettle as the whole street rung again for the weariness thereof' went and 'sat him down quietly upon a block before his own door' when down came the contents of the 'pisse-pot' upon his head: ' "Now, surely", quoth he, "I thought at last that after so great a thunder we should have some rain." ' (*Scatalogical Rites*.)

By the seventeenth century attempts were being made towards a cleaner life. The streets were still filthy, but organised sanitation was slowly improving and efforts being made to channel water more efficiently into towns and cities. For example, in 1609 a new river was brought into London by a Mr Middleton, a goldsmith, who founded the New River Water Company and undertook the enormous task of bringing water some thirty-eight miles from the Chadwell and Anwell Springs in Hertfordshire to reservoirs in Islington, a geographical high point of London. £8,600 was granted by

James I from the Treasury when the finances collapsed half way at Enfield, and work was finished in 1613 when Middleton was knighted.

With the increased availability of water, the water closet was at last to appear. Celia Fiennes saw Queen Anne's at Windsor in the early 1700s: 'within the dressing room is a closet on the one hand, the other side is a closet that leads to a little place with a seat of easement of marble with sluices of water to wash all down.'

The water closet starts to appear in eighteenth-century plans, but with hesitant irregularity; in *Convenient and Ornamental Architecture* by John Crunden, written in 1767, out of the forty-six houses shown, the water closet is recommended for only five. The 'closet' also by now 'a general name for any small room' (*Builders Guide*, 1770) is suggested for only three houses, as is the privy, and one lot of dung holes were thought suitable for a public inn. Adam built a water closet into Shelbourne House in Berkeley Square, two at Osterly with elegant little arched niches of their own and four at Luton Hoo. The water closet was at last in working existence. This was a primitive apparatus, made of marble, with a long handle attached to a plug which you simply pulled up to release the contents of the vessel into the D trap – a D-shaped container filled with water which had another pipe leading out from the top of it, which of course was never emptied properly. These water closets were the first in a long line of inventions, developments and improvements that were to slowly change the unpleasant sanitary habits that still existed in the eighteenth century.

Many of the streets went on being the receptacles and reservoirs for the contents of the chamber pot and the slop pail, despite the fact that drains and sewers were being built and that householders were now allowed to connect their private pipes, leaden for the cellars and kitchens and wooden for the rest of the house, to the main drains, although often at a price. There were human lavatories who picked their way through the foul streets, men with immense capes that enveloped both the customer and the pail that he carried.

Despite the gradually developing water closet and the hopefully written 'Piss-Pot's Farewell' of 1697, the chamber pot was still the most popular convenience in the eighteenth century:

> Presumptuous pisse-pot, how did'st thou offend ?
> Compelling females on their hams to bend ?
> To kings and queens we humbly bend the knee,
> But queens themselves are forced to stoop to thee.
> (*Scatalogical Rites*)

Pots by now were being disguised into the elegance of a piece of furniture; a chair or a chest of drawers. Chippendale, Hepplewhite and Sheraton all designed bedroom cupboards, commodes and shaving tables with ingeniously concealed pots smoothly forming part of them.

Swift despised the pot in the bed chamber or the dark, dank closet: in his *Direction to Servants* of 1745, he writes for the housemaid: 'I am very much offended with those Ladies, who are so proud and lazy, that they will not be at the pains of stepping into the garden to pluck a rose, but keep an odious implement, sometimes in the bedchamber itself, or at least in a dark closet adjoining, which they make use of to ease their worst necessaties; and you are the usual carriers away of the pan, which maketh not only the chamber, but even their clothes offensive, to all who come near. Now, to cure them of the odious practice, let me advise you, on whom this office lieth, to convey away this utensil, that you will do it openly, down the great stairs, and in the presence of the footmen: and, if anybody knocketh, to open the street door, while you have the vessel in your hands: this, if anything can, will make your lady take the pains of evacuating her person in the proper place, rather than expose her filthiness to all the men servants in the house.'

Swift built two water closets himself as early as 1729 which he dramatised in 'The Pangyrick of the Dean' as being his only achievement of lasting value. It is as if written from Lady Acheson, his grateful friend in whose house they were built.

> Two temples of Magnifick Size,
> Attract the curious Trav'llers Eyes,
> That might be envy'd by the Greeks
> Rais'd up by you in twenty weeks:
> Here, gentle Goddess Cloacine
> Receives all Off'rings at her Shrine,
> In sep'rate cells the He's and She's
> Here pay their vows with bended knees:
> (For, 'tis prophane when Sexes mingle;
> And ev'ry Nymph must enter single;
> And when she feels an inward Motion,
> Comes fill'd with Rev'rence and Devotion).
> The bashful Maid, to hide her Blush;
> Shall creep no more behind a Bush;
> Here unobserv'd, she boldly goes,
> As who should say, to Pluck a Rose.

A rose could literally be plucked, as many privies were still being built outside in the eighteenth century, crude structures for the less well-to-do and elegant little temples enhancing the garden for the prosperous. An outside privy by Hawksmoor still survives in the rectory garden of Christ

Church, Spitalfields in Fournier Street, London. William Morris was later to enjoy the pleasures of such a building – which had three seats, at Kelmscott in Gloucestershire. There were one, and one-and-a-half seaters (with a smaller seat for a child), two, three, four, five and six seaters, but by the middle of the century, the water closet was slowly being incorporated inside the grander houses.

Baths too were an important development of the eighteenth century. Baths and bathhouses, little ornate buildings with cosy fireplaced rooms, were built in the grounds of large houses. These depended on either rivers or springs for their water source or upon the tide as at Antony in Cornwall where the small blind arched classical building of 1770 has a plunge pool, open to the skies and three quarters roofed in, in the style of a Roman atrium.

The eighteenth century saw the rise of spa bathing and in *Humphrey Clinker* by Smollett, written between 1768 and 1770, Lydia Melford writes to Miss Willis of the bathers: 'Right under the pump room windows is the Kings bath, a huge cistern where you see the patients up to their necks in hot water. The ladies wear jackets and petticoats of brown linen, with chip hats in which they fix their handkerchieves to wipe the sweat from their faces. . . . My aunt, who says every person of fashion should make her appearance in the bath, as well as in the Abbey Church, contrived a cap with cherry coloured ribbons to suit her complexion.'

Despite these improvements the eighteenth century was still a dirty age. There were very few private baths though people had started to wash in little tin baths in front of the bedroom fire. Some of these baths were most curiously shaped, like boots in which you sat with your head sticking out of the ankle. There were as yet hardly any water closets and the privy and the chamber pot still prevailed. The gentlemen had even managed to get them into their dining rooms for immediate convenience, as well as into their drawing and smoking rooms; behind shutters and curtains, disguised as pieces of furniture and in their sideboard cupboards. Horace Walpole tells a delightful story of Lord Hervey, the Lord Privy Seal, who sought relief behind such a curtain in the room where the ladies were playing cards. He emerged and 'being extremely absent and deep in politics he produced himself in a situation extremely diverting to the women, imagine his delicacy and the extreme passion he was in at their laughing.'

The emptying of these receptacles was a great embarrassment too, as shown by Swift again in his *Directions to Servants*. In the town it was at its worst with both the pots and the buckets being paraded through the house for their contents to be collected by the night soil men. In the 1770s an invention was patented that was, by its example, eventually to put an end to this repellent and unhealthy state of affairs: in 1775 Alexander Cummings, a watch and clockmaker, took out the first patent for a water closet – 'a water closet upon a new construction' – with the important feature of the S trap, the like of which had never been made before. It was to be improved two years later by Thomas Prosser who flattered himself that the 'different noblemen and gentlemen in the three kingdoms, having used them with satisfaction, will be the means of promoting them'. (Patents description.) In 1778 this invention was again altered and perfected by Joseph Bramah and was to remain the most satisfactory water closet for the next ninety-eight years. By 1797 Bramah was claiming to have made and sold six thousand of these closets, and the quality of his workmanship had become so high that the words 'a Bramah' came to be an expression for anything of first rate quality.

The next water closet to be invented was the 'Pan', a repulsive and unsatisfactory arrangement that was to be alternately praised, 'Nothing comes up to the construction . . . which is called the pan closet' (*Walsh's Domestic Economy*) and abhorred by the sanitarians of the day, a new breed of men that developed to meet the needs of the nineteenth century and who were to change our everyday lives to an enormous degree by their efforts of invention and device. S. Stevens Hellyer, whose words are full of excellent, colourful and funny descriptions, who wrote several books, developed water closets, gave lectures, wrote pamphlets galore and ran the successful firm of Dent and Hellyer which still survives today, was one such sanitarian. Typical of his prose is a description of how a water closet could have been tracked down in a hotel before the new sanitary age had dawned: 'Under the old system these sanitary conveniences generally advertised themselves, especially in hotels and places of that kind, and all that one had to do in such buildings was to follow the scent like a hound after a fox, by the dictates of an organ which is very useful, but which one does not care to abuse in such a way, for, to say the least, it is an offensive way to follow up a thing.'

It is not recorded when the Pan was invented but it is known to have been 'improved' in 1796 by William Law: This too was a foul contraption. Bramah's valve was consistently in the background, setting a shining example, but one that was never successfully taken up, although there were several cheap imitators, as it was so expensive to produce. The 'Hopper' came next, a simple coneshaped vessel in earthenware or iron that went straight down into the trap. The surface area was too large for the trickling spiral of water to deal with and it was never properly cleaned. 'There is left a "fixture",' wrote Hellyer, the hero of sanitary prose, 'like the basin itself which the outgoing tenant is generous enough to leave behind him for the in-coming tenant to see, and have the benefit of, without anything to pay.' (*Principals and Practices of Plumbing*, 1891.)

There were many other sanitary heroes in the nineteenth century; inventors, engineers, producers, manufacturers and politicians, who had to fight the clogged inertia of sanitary reform. Mr S.R. Bostel can remember his grandfather Daniel Thomas Bostel, the first successful producer of the wash-out W.C. in 1875, telling him of the embarrassment suffered by Victorian ladies when faced with the water closet at exhibitions. 'They would blush and turn away', for them it was like looking at a huge and glistening naked behind.

Despite the fact that a Chancellor of the Exchequer was reported in *The Builder* of July 1851 to have made the daring statement that 'Sanitary Reform is a humbug', the reformers struggled on; the Reverend Charles Kingsley, author of *The Water Babies*, preached that disease was God's punishment to the populace for leading so repulsive an existence: 'Filthy and unwholesome habits of living are in the sight of almighty God so terrible and offensive, that He sometimes finds it necessary to visit them with a severity with which he visits hardly any sin; namely, by inflicting capital punishment on thousands of His beloved creatures.'

In 1848 a new public health act was passed making it obligatory for a fixed sanitary arrangement of some kind; an ash pit, a privy or a water closet, to be fitted by every householder. The Metropolitan Commissioners for Sewers, founded in 1847, abolished all cesspits.

In 1858 the Metropolitan Board of Works was founded, which, with Sir Joseph Bazalgette, began the enormous undertaking of laying a new sewerage system beneath London in 1859. Over one thousand miles of sewers were to be built and the grand scheme was finished in 1865. London was at last becoming a healthier place to live in and the rest of the country did not lag behind.

It was George Jennings who first applied the new sanitary technology to public conveniences. He had introduced his ideas at the Great Exhibition of 1851, with his 'Monkey closets' (forerunners of the 'wash-out') in the 'retiring rooms' both at Hyde Park and later at Sydenham. This was despite the strongest objections, with him being told that the visitors were not coming to the exhibition merely to wash. He was later to be awarded a gold medal for this much needed work and by the 1890s – progress in this field was slow – Jennings and his followers had improved the public thoroughfares all over England: thirty-six towns and 'many others' are listed in his catalogue of 1895 as having been improved by public

conveniences. He had also supplied them to thirty railway companies in England, one in America, and to others in Buenos Aires, Cape Town and Mexico. The streets of Paris, Berlin and Florence were provided with Jennings' public urinals, as were those of Madrid, Frankfurt, Soulina, Hong Kong and Sydney, New South Wales.

Jennings' ideas were revolutionary: firstly many conveniences were built underground, with cast iron arches, railings or pergolas to mark their whereabouts. Those built above ground were distinctive little buildings in their own right with their finials, pillars, panels and enhancing lamps. He built the urinals themselves in slate, and he also devised the central pillar with urinals around it, that is so economical with both space and water.

Jennings' catalogues have superb drawings of the urinals in the townscape, usually with a darkened figure emerging, adjusting himself, to remind you of what you are looking at. They are little temples of convenience enhancing wherever they stand. A stirring poem was written to commemorate the opening of Jennings' first public convenience:

> I' front the Royal Exchange and Underground
> Down gleaming walls of porc'lain flows the sluice
> That out of sight decants the Kidney Juice,
> Thus pleasuring those Gents for miles around,
> Who, crying for relief, once piped the sound,
> Of wind in alley-ways. All hail this news!
> And let the joyous shuffling queues
> For Gentlemanly Jennings' most well found
> Construction, wherein a penny opes the gate
> To Heav'n's mercy and Sanitary waves
> Receive the Gush with seemingly, cool obedience,
> Enthroning Queen Hygeia in blessed state
> On Crapper's Rocket: with raptuous ease men's cares
> Shall flow away when seated at convenience!
>
> (*The Good Loo Guide*)

Such reform was far from absolute in the home, the water closet, flushing efficiently might be found in one house, whilst next door the only convenience could be the bog house at the bottom of the garden. For washing and bathing the 'lavatory' (washbasin) with its framed mirror rising above it, had developed into an object of grace by the 1880s, enormous and flowering like a fruit tree trained flat against a garden wall. Similarly immense canopied baths, little houses of carved wooden panels, were starting to appear in some households, whilst at Belvoir Castle, for example, all washing was done with the jugs and basins of the wash stand and with the tin hip bath in front of the fire. Baths were not installed at Belvoir until 1912.

The gas heated bath of 1871 seems to have been a terrifying alternative with naked flames of gas burning beneath an ornate metal tub. One called the 'General Gordon Gas Bath' had a little pinnacled canister connected to it, on which you put your towels to warm. There was a hinged bunsen burner which you swung under the bath once the flames were lit, but as there was no flue, the combination of the scorching hot metal and the gas vapours must have made taking such a bath a misery.

Other closet inventions were appearing all the time and from the 1840s several patents for water closets were taken out and published, for example in *The Builder*. In 1844 a 'portable closet' with a little cistern of water all neatly enclosed with the bowl in a wooden chest was brought onto the market patented by a Mr Wiss near Charing Cross. It was taken up and sold by all the suppliers until the end of the century. The Reverend Moule's 'Earth Closet' appears to be the next major development; it was a curious contraption for so late a date, 1860, but again proved to be a great success. It was based on the principle that dry and sifted earth is an excellent deodoriser and, that however many times it is used, when dry, its power is as good as ever. The earth, in a cone behind the seat, was released in a measured quantity when you pulled the handle. No supply of water was needed and the sewers would therefore not be contaminated. The use of excretia of the "paragon of animals" was advocated by Dr Vivian Poore in 1897 in his book *The Dwelling House*. He had 'rather handsomely manured his garden with human excretia' and recommended the earth closet, the dry catch and the pail method. At the time of writing, the ecological closet has a respectable following. With a clatlava tree growing nearby, whose leaves you use instead of paper, it consists of a box containing a compost heap providing the optimum conditions for breaking down human refuse into by-products.

Water closets, baths and 'lavatories' (washbasins) were to become decorated and beautiful objects for the twenty-five years between 1875 and 1900. They appeared in a dazzling variety of patterns with names like 'Ruby Hispani', 'Natural Wild Rose and Pencilled Blackthorn', 'Peacock Blue Poppy' and 'Japanesque'. The men responsible for this decorative explosion were responsible too, during these twenty-five years, for developing the water closet system as we know it today.

It seems to have been the Prince of Wales' near death from typhoid in 1871 – Prince Albert had died from the disease in 1861 – that jolted public feelings on sanitary reform. The Prince himself had been so stirred by the possible consequences of bad drains that he declared that he should like to be a plumber if he were not a prince. Certainly, it was from

this point that domestic sanitary reform flourished. Hellyer for example improved Bramah's valve closet some hundred years after it had been invented, with his 'Optimus'. He produced sixteen of them with slight variations in their workings ranging from the 'Optimus A' to the 'Optimus P'. 'They have several imitators, but still remain – OPTIMUS.' (Dent and Hellyer advertisement.) Among the improvements was the flushing rim, 'I have great difficulty in getting potters to make it'. The Optimus, produced up until the outbreak of the Second World War, could boast of a most distinguished patronage: They were installed in Buckingham Palace, Windsor Castle, Hampton Court Palace, Holyrood House and Osborne for Queen Victoria, in Marlborough House, Windsor, Buckingham Palace and Balmoral for Edward VII. They were also installed for George V, the Czar of Russia, the King of Siam and the Duke of Wellington and in the Houses of Parliament, the Royal Courts of Justice and the War Office.

Hellyer claimed to have invented the 'wash-out' closet after having seen Jennings' 'Monkey Closet' but none appear to have survived and no more was written of them elsewhere. Daniel Thomas Bostel, however, was exhibiting his 'Excelsior' wash-out as early as 1875 and his grandson Mr S.R. Bostel can still show you an example of the ceramic pedestal closet today. The next wash-out to appear, this time with its workings hidden away by a wooden enclosure, was the 'National' by Thomas Twyford in 1881, which was such a commercial success that by 1889 Twyfords could claim that a hundred thousand were in use. It was followed by an all ceramic pedestal version in 1883, the 'Unitas', which was brought out initially with an oak tree, in relief, growing up to the bowl. 'Unlike ordinary W.C. basins it is not enclosed with woodwork but is fully exposed, so that no filth nor anything causing offensive smells can accumulate or escape detection.' There were a number of tests devised at this time to find out where escaping odours were coming from: the peppermint test, the gas test, the ether, the ammonia and the smoke test. Cannisters on long handles with the oils, liquids, gases or smoke inside them were thrust between the two traps and the points of the escaping fumes could then be tracked down.

Edward Johns was another sanitary innovator who in 1896 made one of the finest W.C.s of all, which is sadly no longer surviving, the Lion on whose back you sat on a handsome key pattened bowl. This firm later became Armitage Ware. John Shanks was another of the great sanitary figures who, by 1864, had patented his first W.C. – an improved version of the old plunger closet with the additions of a valve and ballcock, which came to be known as 'No. 4'. At the first testing of his No. 4, Shanks had apparently seized a cap off a workman's head and flung it into the water, shouting, 'It works!' as the cap flushed away. By 1895, when he died, the business had become a world wide concern, making beautiful baths, water closets and lavatories, and as with Twyfords, the catalogues of what was produced astound one with the quality of workmanship, inventiveness and imagination and as too with Twyfords, the catalogues themselves are like illuminated manuscripts.

Doultons another firm which became a household name in the history of sanitation also produced these exquisite books. Their catalogue of 1916 could boast: 'A few important sanitary installations in India and Burma: the Vice Regal Lodge, Delhi, the residences of the governors of Madras, Bombay, the Punjab, Behar and Orissa and Bengal, the High Courts in Delhi and seven palaces.'

George Jennings was one of the first and one of the greatest of these innovators in the world of sanitary reform, as early as 1847 Prince Albert had presented him with the medal of the Society of Arts. Jennings fitted up the hospitals at Scutari and Varna, he supervised the sanitary arrangements at the service for the recovery of the Prince of Wales at St. Pauls. He provided the Empress Eugenie with a copper bath, and supplied the ex-Kedive of Egypt with a great multi-showered mahogany canopied contraption. He devised a bath for hospital and asylums with a lever acting supply valve that ensured that the hot water could never be let into the bath, unless the cold was first and proportionately turned on. He patented tip up basins that swivelled round on an axle to be emptied, and of course, his syphonic 'Closet of the Century'. J.R. Mann had already patented the syphonic system in 1870 but with no great success and Jennings' improvements made the syphonic one of the most prestigious lavatories of its time.

We have George Jennings to thank for producing the direct descendant of our lavatories today, with the syphonic 'Closet of the Century', and also the firm of Humpherson & Co. of Chelsea for first patenting the wash-down with their 'Beaufort' in 1884. The firm had been founded by Edward Humpherson in 1876, who was later joined by his two sons Frederick and Alfred, who had each served four-year apprenticeships with Thomas Crapper at his Marlborough Works in Chelsea. Humpherson's at their Beaufort Works produced a number of patented inventions winning prizes and medals at exhibitions, but their greatest achievement of all was the Beaufort of which so many millions have since been copied. The firm is still a successful one today with Edward Humpherson's great-grandson Geoffrey Pidgeon as chairman.

Thomas Crapper, nearby, was in constant professional rivalry with Humpherson. His main interest was with cisterns and water waste preventers although he did supply a lavatory emblazoned with the Prince of Wales' feathers, which was supposedly allowed when he had been given the Royal Warrant after he had installed the drains and sanitary fittings at Sandringham between 1886 and 1909.

Between them all these firms produced hundreds of innovations and variations on the water closet. Today only four are made: the wash-down and the syphonic, the squatting bowl and the wash-out for suppliers abroad. There were 'Trapless Twin Basin' closets, 'Ventilating Pan' closets, 'Treadle Action', 'Pneumatic' and 'Pneumatic Combinations'. There was the 'Elastic Valve', the 'Flusherette Valve', the 'Valve Hopper' and the 'Pan Valve', the 'Trapless Valve', the 'Water Battery', the closet with the self-acting seat and numerous self-acting closets.

The astonishing thing is that all this happened so recently, the lavatory as we know it today was invented within living memory. Since the 1880s they have changed neither their workings nor their basic shape. The cantilevered water closet was already being advertised in all the catalogues of the 1890s, and modernisation has simply meant a mean streamlining of what was once a rich, delightful and enjoyable form. The lavatory is an intimate friend to us all, and we should honour it as such. It is undeniable that a glorious throne with a welcoming wooden seat makes us laugh with pleasure, why then do we minimise its importance, making it a mere receptacle, a necessary evil? But there is a ray of hope, after seventy years of sterile sanitary design architects such as John Prizeman, realising the 'sheer solid joy' that a well-designed lavatory and a capacious bath can give, are once again planning temples in which we can luxuriate.

THE TWO MAJOR TYPES OF WATER CLOSET MECHANISM

There are two types of water closets; mechanical and non-mechanical. With the mechanical the arrangement for controlling the flush is in close connection with the basin, forming part of it. With the non-mechanical all the controlling parts are contained in the cistern, leaving the closet below more reliable and easier to manufacture.

Mechanical – valve, pan, plug and twin basin.

Non-mechanical – hopper, wash-out, wash-down and syphonic.

1. The latrine, around which as many as twenty men could sit side by side, at Housteads, the immense fort on the Roman Wall in Northumberland. There was a continuous wooden bench into which holes were carved boxed in over the deeply dug outer sewer. At the sitters' feet was a smaller channel into which they dipped their unappealingly communal sponge sticks, used instead of paper. By means of a clever internal pipe, these channels were supplied with rain water from the stone tanks nearby.

2

3

2. The Great Bath at Aqua Sulis (Bath) built by the Romans in the second century A.D. and abandoned by them two hundred years later. It was not until the 1870s, when some buildings were demolished, that they were discovered and then gradually restored over the next twenty-six years. The lead pipe in the foreground is original but everything above the column bases dates from the nineteenth century.

3. The fifteenth-century lavatorium of Gloucester Cathedral which is a miniature version of the staggering fan vaulted cloisters next to which it stands. Originally the trough was lead lined with the water in lead tanks ranged along the back.

4. Late fifteenth-century garderobe at Cleeve Abbey in Somerset, built into the thickness of the breast which supported the frater pulpit above.

5. Part of the twelfth-century laver, once a great carved enclosed circular shrine to cleanliness, at Much Wenlock Priory in Shropshire.

6. Nine arches for nine latrines, enhancing Fountains Abbey in Yorkshire. They were built between 1160 and 1180 with probably twice as many again built back to back above them, for the lay brothers, between their dormitory and infirmary.

7. A medieval lavabo with a curious carving of a dog chewing a bone, in the undercroft of Wells Cathedral. It could be of any date between 1170 and 1320 when work on the undercroft was finished.

8. The grotesque open-mouthed face through which all the filth flowed from a garderobe. This one is at Beaumaris Castle on the island of Anglesey, North Wales, built by Edward I between 1295–1330.

9. No less than three garderobes and two latrines can be seen in this photograph. The Keep, originally built in the mid thirteenth century, was surrounded by a wall, in which two latrines still survive with their outlets cut into the rock down to the moat below. The slit for a window in the foreground was the only other means of ventilation. The three projecting garderobes date from the early sixteenth century when the upper stages of the Keep were reconstructed. Greencastle in County Down, Northern Ireland.

10

11

13

12

10. One of the two two-seater garderobes in the scrupulously restored Haddon Hall in Derbyshire. Beneath the seats is a drop of some thirty feet onto a steep slope of rock where either the rain or an unfortunate 'menial' cleaned everything away.

11. What was originally a five-seater privy in the early-seventeenth-century garden wall of The Deanery, Staindrop, County Durham. It was remodelled in the nineteenth century as a two-seater with oak panelling.

12. The Duchess of Lauderdale's close stool of about 1675 in the ante-chamber to the Queen's bedchamber at Ham House. In the inventory of 1679 the Green Drawing Room was recorded to contain 'in the closset' one japanned close stool box. Such a discreet compartment was variously called the 'close stool house', the 'house of office', or 'le lieu', in many seventeenth-century plans.

13. A six-seater at Chilthorne Dormer Manor, near Yeovil in Somerset from the late seventeenth to mid eighteenth century. The seats go round the wall of a small pyramid roofed stone house in the garden. Mr Eric Northrop of the Science Museum Annexe at Hayes remembers the terrible shock of going into the six-seater public convenience at the Cattle Market in Belfast in 1937. There were six farmers, all with their trousers down, sitting reading broadsheet newspapers, two by two, each man holding one page.

14 and 15. A Royal close stool covered in red velvet with a stuffed horse-hair seat that was probably used by Charles I and Charles II and certainly by James II, at Knole near Sevenoaks in Kent. It is thought to have been brought here from either Hampton Court or Whitehall Palace by the 6th Earl of Dorset who, when appointed Lord Chamberlain to William and Mary, was allowed the established prerequisite of removing the state furniture of the previous monarch to his own home.

16. The Sunderland Ware chamber pot belonging to
the Duke of Wellington at Stratfield Saye.
Sunderland Ware from Sunderland in County
Durham was in its commercial heyday in 1840 when
there were as many as twenty-four factories making
the china. They were renowned for their lustre ware
and had a most curious speciality: religious tracts,
gilded and lustred on china plaques, a far cry from
the verses that elegantly decorate the outside of this
pot!

Under the heading 'Marriage':
   This pot it is a Present sent
   Some mirth to make is only meant,
   We hope the same, you'll not refuse
   But keep it safe and oft it use.
   When in it you want to p:ss
   Remember them who sent you THIS.
Under the heading 'Present':
   Dear lovely wife pray rise and p:ss
   Take you that handle and I'll take this
   Let's use the present which was sent
   To make some mirth is only meant
   So let it be as they have said.
   We'll laugh and P:ss and then to Bed.

17 and 18. Wooden two and three seaters, curiously similar, twenty miles apart
from each other in East Anglia. The two seater is at Thorpe Hall, Horham near

19. The water closet in the Turrett Room at Osterley in Middlesex. The house, originally built by Sir Thomas Gresham in the mid sixteenth century, was transformed into a curious classical palace by Robert Adam in 1762. There has always been a water closet in this niche in the Turrett Room. It is recorded that a carpenter, Matthew Hillyard, fitted one there as early as 1756. Dent and Hellyer installed an 'Optimus' (E) valve closet shown in the photograph in 1879 though the niche is as Adam decorated it.

Eye, the three seater at Hempnall's Hall, Cotton near Stowmarket. Both are pine and could be of any date from the early eighteenth to the late nineteenth century.

20. The rare and extraordinary eighteenth-century Chinese dressing room at Saltram, near Plymouth in Devon. The wallpaper dates from the reign of K'ang Hsi (1662–1722) and was put up when Saltram was finished in 1756. This date is precise as a surplus bit of the paper was used as a backing for the Chippendale mirror which was delivered that year. It is therefore one of the earliest Chinese wallpapers still surviving in England.

The cans for hot and cold water, the bath and the foot bath are Victorian. The wig stand in the corner dates from the early nineteenth century, originally used to powder wigs over the bowl it was undoubtedly later used as a wash stand.

21. The five-and-a-half-feet deep by twelve-feet wide marble bath built for Lord Clive (of India) in the early 1770s at Claremont, Esher, in Surrey. It is in the basement at Claremont in a little vaulted room (which is now an office). A wrought iron railing was once fixed to either end of the bath. The cost of this and the plumbing came to £310 15s 3d (£310.76). (By courtesy of the Governors and Headmistress of Claremont School.)

22. A late-eighteenth to early-nineteenth-century pine column commode at Raby Castle in County Durham.

23. The lower part of a pan closet of about 1790, originally at Hampton Court, now in the Science Museum, London. Complete, it would have had a basin above the container and pan.

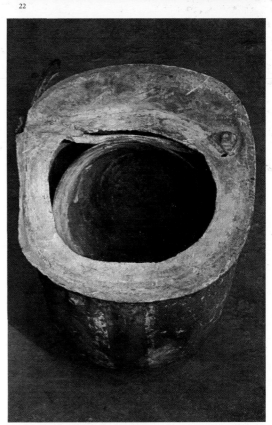

24 and 25. Late-eighteenth to early-nineteenth-century pine commode in simulated bamboo with false drawer front, photographed at Debenham in Suffolk. It had become very popular by the eighteenth century to hide away the pot into the elegance of a piece of furniture.

Why Strephon will you tell the rest?
And must you needs describe the Chest?
That careless Wench! no Creature warn her
To move it out from yonder Corner;
But leave it standing full in Sight
For you to exercise your Spight.
In vain, the Workman shew'd his Wit
With Rings and Hinges counterfeit
To make it seem in this Disguise,
A Cabinet to vulgar Eyes;
Which Strephon ventured to look in,
Resolv'd to go through thick and thin;
He lifts the Lid, there need no more,
He smelt it all the Time before.

JONATHAN SWIFT
'The Lady's Dressing Room'

26. The soap dish of a nineteenth-century transfer printed washbasin at Thorpe Hall, near Diss, in Norfolk. The design was applied in the biscuit stage and the extra embellishment painted on by hand.

27. 'New Marble in Silver grey', a washbasin of the late 1800s made by Edward Johns and Company Limited, now Armitage Ware Ltd, Staffordshire.

28. 'New Marble in Rouge Royal', a washbasin of 1896 made by Edward Johns and Company Limited now in Armitage Shanks showroom, Staffordshire.

29. A washhandstand designed by William Burges in the 1860s for his rooms in Buckingham Street and later given by Sir John Betjeman to Evelyn Waugh in 1953. It is the first washhandstand to be made by Burges in this shape with slender square cut legs supporting a cupboard with carved and massively hinged doors that conceal the waste tank beneath the basin. From the two lead-lined tanks behind the frieze, one for hot and the other for cold water, a little dragon-like creature head spouts into the bowl below.

30. The third Marquis of Bute's washbasin of about 1868 in the Batchelor bedroom in the Clock Tower at Cardiff Castle. William Burges, the architect, and Lord Bute, his exceedingly rich young patron, were both ardent and imaginative medievalists who decided in 1865 to restore and rebuild Cardiff Castle. (By kind permission of the City of Cardiff.)

31. A Shanks 'Cast iron Lavatory Stand' of the 1890s, in Lady Bullough's bathroom at Kinloch Castle on the island of Rhum. In Shanks' catalogue of 1899 it is listed as costing £7 14s (£7.70). This included the cast iron stand, the 'Modern' 'Lavatory', the four tiles above the taps (which could be decorated), the shelf and bracket and the mirror which was magnificently framed, japanned and decorated.

32. The ladies retiring room at Harrods in London, built in 1908 as part of a suite of sumptuous rooms for the Ladies Club. The windows are of stained Cathedral glass, while the walls are covered throughout with panelled Brecchi Sanguine, Pavannazi, Levantine marble and onyx panels. Surprisingly Harrods gets most of its water supply from a private well.

33. A washbasin at Mount Stuart on the Isle of Bute, the splendid fantasy house built for the third Marquis of Bute by Sir Rowland Anderson between the 1880s–90s.

34. Lady Bute's washstand thought to be designed by John Chapple in a room designed by William Burges, at Castell Coch, Glamorganshire. The turrets are functional: both are lead lined, one is for hot water and the other for cold. (Having been brought up a good many extremely steep stairs in two buckets!) The fish tap emblazoned with the coronet and the letter B spouts water onto the china fish swimming round in the china tip-up basin.

35. The gentlemen's cloakroom in the Manchester Club, formerly the Reform Club, built by Edward Salomons, 1870–71. This fine room is of a later date, when some interior changes were made in the mid 1890s. The sanitary fittings are by Doultons. On the washbasin at the end of the room there is a curious pump-like pipe, on which are written the words: 'This water is delivered absolutely pure by the Berkeld Filter. 21 Oxford Street.' To the right of this basin is a marble partition to give privacy to those cleaning their false teeth.

36. Edward VII's urinal at Wolferton Royal Railway Station, built by the Great Eastern Railway on the Sandringham Estate in Norfolk. Between the years 1898 – when this part of the station was completed – and 1907, the station-master's diary records amongst other visitors the names of the crowned heads of Europe that passed through Wolferton: the German Emperor was there in 1899 and 1902, King Carlos of Portugal in 1902, the King of the Hellenes in 1905 and the King of Spain in 1907, and as likely as not all of them passed through this cloakroom as well. The basin, a Jennings 'club pattern', was specially decorated for the Prince of Wales with dark blue and gold lines.

For 37/– (£1.85) to go with this urinal, you could buy the singular 'Treadle Action Supply Apparatus', a small, galvanised iron plinth decorated with tiles on which you stood 'flushing a continuous flush to the urinal basin whilst in use'.

37. One of the many WCs disguised as wardrobes – there is a little fully furnished room with a valve closet behind each door – that were ordered by the Duke of Wellington in 1841 for Stratfield Saye near Reading. In 1823 the servants had had to be asked not to empty their pots into the gutters at the top of the house so terrible had been the stench. The Duke was by this time discussing the possibilities of installing a water closet, but it was not until 1841 that these magnificently entranced chambers were designed. There were eight put in that year. The architect Benjamin Dean Wyatt seems to have been delighted, he wrote to the Duke whilst they were being made: 'My Lord, I have been today to inspect the outside cases for the several closets . . . The Canadian wood (which they call ''Rock Marble'') turns out the handsomest wood for such a purpose, that I ever saw in my life, and I rather believe that the two casings which have been made of it, are the only example of it in England.'

38. 'The Ladies Club' at Harrods in London with the walnut and marquetry doors marching down the full length of this extraordinarily elaborate 'retiring room', built in 1908.

WASHROOM

39 and 40. The gentleman's convenience at Market Place, Hull, built in 1901–2. B. Finch and Co. Limited Sanitary Engineers, Lambeth supplied all the sanitary fittings: there are eleven 'marbled' slate urinal stalls, two delightful cisterns, 'marble flush tanks with bevelled glass fronts, copper cylinders and polished gun metal traps, fixed on marble cantilevers', on the front of these were two tiny grey marble Tuscan pillars, 'Finch's 3-range lavatory marble tops' and six Finch's syphonic closets with mahogany seats. The total building costs came to £1,129. The tiles, the convenience's most distinctive feature, came to a mere £90.

41. Twenty Twyford 'St Ann's Marble' urinal stalls surrounding the magnificent 'Hexagonal Adamant Urinal Range' on the pier at Rothesay Harbour, Bute, built in 1889.

42. The magnificent faience and tile work of the gentleman's cloakroom of what was the City Club, now the City of London Club, in Old Broad Street, built in 1907 at a total cost of over £6,000.

43. The urinals, part of a range of eight, under the deep faience frieze in the gentleman's cloakroom, of the City of London Club. The urinals, slate bottomed cisterns, the 'Sylph Syphonic' closets and the 'Lavazonic' washbasins were all supplied by Matthew Hall and Company of Wigmore Street, London in 1902, a firm that still survives today in Tottenham Court Road.

44. One of the two ceramic arches by Willink and Thicknesse that stand at entrances to the gentleman's underground convenience in Derby Square, Liverpool. They were built as an adjunct to an immense monument to Queen Victoria who stands directly above them.

45. Twyford's 'Rouge Royal' urinals and cistern, in the gents of the Philharmonic Public House, Hope Street, Liverpool. These circular backed urinals were available from Twyford's stock with sage green pillars and tops, and white backs, at the price per person of £11. 'Rouge Royal' and 'Rich brown' could be ordered 'at an extra, according to treatment'. The process of marbling used by all the potters was the same – the patterns were transfer printed onto the biscuit (fired but unglazed pottery) and the ware was then passed through a hardening-on kiln before glazing.

47

46. One of the three cast iron urinals put up at Great Ayton in Yorkshire in 1902, at a cost of £15, probably by Lockerbie Wilkinson of Exeter Street, Birmingham.

47 and 48. A bee for men to aim at to avoid splashing (the Latin for bee is *apis*). One of two 'Diamond' urinals in leadless glaze designed by Walter E. Mason of Harwich in Lancashire, between 1878 and 1882, for the Wigan College of Technology, Library Street, Wigan. Messrs Twyfords at one time manufactured an urinal stall with a bullseye under the glaze.

48

49. The Old Toll bar, Paisley Road West, Glasgow, built in 1896.

50. The gents door of the Horseshoe bar in Drury Street, Glasgow, built in the 1870s by architects Peddie and Kinnear of Edinburgh.

51

◁51. Queen Victoria's water closet in the 1869 Royal Compartment of the London and North-Western Railway. Part of the sumptuous suite designed for her by William Bore. The cloakroom between the bedroom and the drawing room is very small, just the width of the closet seat. (The photograph is taken looking into the mirror on the inside of the door.) It is a valve closet with a delicately painted key pattern in turquoise and gold around the bowl.

52. The closet in the Royal Compartment of the London and North-Western Railway made for John Brown, the dour Scots ghillie who became Queen Victoria's personal attendant in 1865. The two royal coaches bulge with splendour, all Victorian dreams of luxury, opulence and grandeur are stuffed into them.

53

54

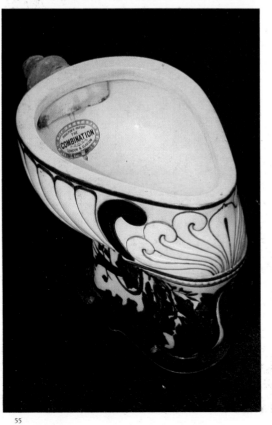

53. The 'Westminster Portcullis', a wash-down closet at the showrooms of Humpherson and Company, London.

54. Doultons 'Lambeth Patent Pedestal "Combination" flush-out closet' in 'Raised Acanthus, picked out in blue' at Hordley, near Wootton in Oxfordshire.

55. 'The Lambeth Patent Pedestal "Combination" Closet', a wash-out in 'Blue Magnolia' at Pownall Hall, Wilmslow in Cheshire.

56. The 'Empire', a wash-down closet made by Edward Johns principally for the Canadian market. Its trap outlet is through the floor and the pipe goes on down to the basement – a frost proof necessity against the Canadian weather, which a standard outside stack pipe would not be able to stand up to. (Gladstone Pottery Museum, Longton, Stoke-on-Trent.)

55

56

57. The queen of water closets, the 'Unitas' in 'Raised oak' design possibly the most beautiful basin of all. Invented by Thomas Twyford in 1883 the 'Unitas' was one of the first all-ceramic pedestal wash-out closets with the enormous advantage of not being boxed in where it would accumulate dirt all the while. This splendid 1888 basin is extremely rare in that it was decorated inside and out with two separate designs. The 'Unitas' was so successful that by 1901 Twyfords could claim that it 'surpasses in sale and reputation all water closets of this type'.

58

59

60

61

58. A Jennings wash-down closet in 'Morning Glory' pattern. It was removed from the Major's Parlour in Brighton Town Hall during some office reconstruction and is now safely preserved in the Royal Pavilion Art Gallery and Museum.

60. The Waterway, a wash-down WC supplied by W. N. Froy to a house in Fielding Road, London W4.

59. The 'National', one of the first all earthenware wash-out closets, transfer printed with vines, corn and passion flowers. Produced by Thomas Twyford, it won the 'Highest Awards' at 'The International Medical and Sanitary Exhibition' at South Kensington in 1881, and by 1889 100,000 were in use. (Gladstone Pottery Museum, Longton, Stoke-on-Trent.)

61. A wash-out closet in the Science Museum, London, which was removed from the now demolished Redhill House, Edgware, in 1971.

62

63

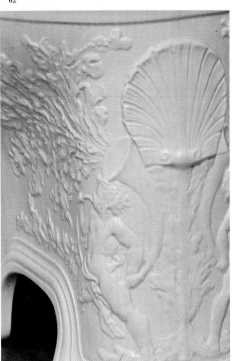

64

65

62. The 'Pilaster', a wash-down closet belonging to Mr and Mrs Walter Caley of Bury St Edmunds in Suffolk.

63. The 'Oeneas' wash-down closet at 37 Bath Road, London W4, designed to West London County Council Regulations.

64. The 'Latestas' wash-down closet of 1899 in the Science Museum Annexe at Hayes. 'Specially suited for London County Council', the workings were designed by a Mr George Davis of the Westminster Sanitary Works, inventor of the first automatically ventilated 'Closet Apartment'. The pedestal was potted by Shanks.

65. The 'Latestas', a wash-down closet produced by George Davis.

67

66. The handsome 'Compactum' combination wash-down closet with 'raised decoration'. Part of the complete Edwardian bathroom that survives in Kinloch Castle on the island of Rhum, built between 1898 and 1902 by Leaming and Leaming. Under the heading 'A New Departure' Shanks' catalogue of 1890 goes on to say: 'This system supplies a long felt want, by combining the closet and the waste-preventing supply cistern in one compact piece; thus saving tremendous labour in fitting up, to a large extent, and avoiding the noise and complications of overhead cisterns . . . everything is within reach'.

67. 'The Citizen' a wash-down combination closet of 1899 in 'Architectural' design in the cloakroom at Kinloch Castle on the island of Rhum.

68. 'The Vaal', with a great carved cistern, produced by the Valveless Syphon Company, Kirkstall, Leeds. A forerunner of the modern 'Lowdown combination suite' (as we choose to call our lavatories today), in that the cistern has been lowered. Until the invention of the syphonic the height of the cistern had been depended upon to give force to the flush. It was Shanks who introduced the Lowdown in the late 1880s. This huge pillar-like closet, no longer used, is hidden away in the labyrinth of attics at Knole in Kent.

68

69. Doultons 'Improved Pedestal "Simplicitas" Wash-Down Closet', in plain stoneware with 'Acanthus Raised Decoration'. The price of a stoneware basin was almost doubled by the opulent addition of this design. For asylums, where 'stoneware' strength was particularly useful, you could order it with a self-lifting seat 'to meet the requirements of the commissioners in lunacy'. (Gladstone Pottery Museum, Longton, Stoke-on-Trent.)

70

71

72

73

70. The Duke of Bedford's private closet in his box at the Royal Opera House, Covent Garden. With wild aspirations to grandeur, Jennings has woven his name: 'George Jennings, Patentee, Hydraulic and Sanitary Engineer, Palace Wharf, London, Stangate, Lambeth' into a seemingly Royal coat of arms.

72. 'The Closet of the Century', made by George Jennings. A particularly finely shaped water closet with a syphonic discharge mechanism, it boasted of having both the advantages of the wash-down and the valve closet. (The force of water in the wash-down, the quietness of action in the valve.) You could buy it in both the enclosed and pedestal form. This design was the only gold medal at the Manchester Health Exhibition of 1894 and the Grand Prix at Paris in 1900. The closet illustrated here is at Rousham Park near Oxford.

71. 'Panorama' design giving unexpected grandeur to a 'Hopper' closet the cheapest and most humble of systems. This basin plumbed up to date and built into a handsome modern walnut enclosure belongs to Lord Londonderry.

73. 'Best Quality' valve closet made by H. Pontifex and Sons Limited at the Farringdon Works Limited, Shoe Lane, London. A curious extra was available with this closet: a 'Looking Glass Bottom Valve' costing 5/– (25p) in 1896. Pontifex would also engrave the customer's name and town on to the handle dish.

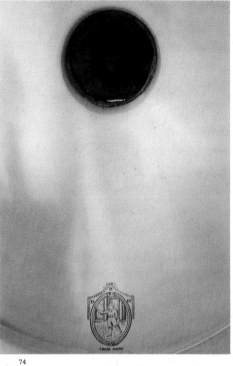

74

75

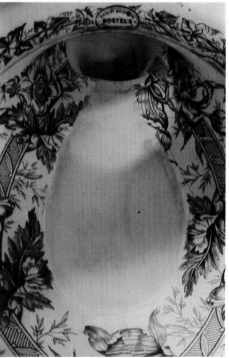

76

74. The water closet in the Turrett Room at Osterley in Middlesex. The 'Plumber's Mate' in breeches walking over cobbles in the badge at the back of the bowl was the trade mark of Dent and Hellyer.

75. One of the two pan closets that are to be found in the woods near the house of Seaforde in County Down, Northern Ireland. Both of the closets have this merry scene of dancing in front on an Italianate house.

76. The first commercially successful wash-out closet produced by Daniel Bostel of Bostel Bros. Ltd of Brighton, and exhibited by him as early as 1875.

77

78

79

80

81

82

77. The 'Tubal' wash-out closet. John Shanks' brother, a religious man, suggested the name 'Tubal' from Tubalcain, described in Genesis, Chapter 4, as an 'instructor of every artificer in brass and iron'. (Armitage Shanks showroom, Staffordshire.)

80. The 'Sultan', a Shanks wash-out closet of 1896 at Wallington Hall, Cambo, Northumberland.

78. The Excelsior, a wash-down WC. the patent for this pattern was taken out in 1895 by The Sanitary Pottery Co, Bournes Bank, Burslem in Staffordshire. (Armitage Shanks showroom, Staffordshire.)

81. 'Not by Appointment to the King', an ingenious sales trick on an Edward Johns 'Dolphin' wash-out closet in 1909.

79. The 'Beaufort', the 'Original Pedestal wash-down closet' made by Humpherson and Company, Beaufort Works, Chelsea, London in 1884.

82. The 'Waterfall' wash-down closet, St Peter's Square, London.

83

85

84. The 'Unitas', with 'Florentine' design, at Croxdale Hall in County Durham, the first ever all ceramic pedestal wash-out closet, invented by Thomas Twyford in 1883.

83. Doulton's 'Improve Pedestal Simplicitas' wash-down closet with 'highly ornamented raised decorations' at Stockport Cricket Club in Cheshire.

85. The 'Deluge', a wash-down closet in the 'Venetian' pattern, by Twyfords in Raby Castle, County Durham. There were twenty-four patterns to choose from to decorate either the 'Deluge', the 'Cardinal' or the 'Sirdar' Twyford wash-down basins.

86. The 'Dolphin', the king of water closets, a wash-out, in this case supplied by Stock Sons and Taylor of Birmingham. It appears in a Bolding catalogue of the early 1880s.

87

88

87. Beleek china chamber pot at Seaforde in County Down, Northern Ireland, most likely to have been manufactured as a protest against Home Rule, with Gladstone to vent your rage on in the bowl. Beleek was produced in County Fermanagh, and the firm is still going strong.

88. A pot now belonging to the Duchess of Wellington at Stratfield Saye. When lifted this 'PATENT NON SPLASH THUNDER BOWL' plays music.

89

90

91

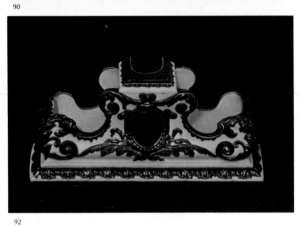

92

89. 1840 Gothic Revival commode, with a comfortable green felt seat, and matching washstand at Raby Castle in County Durham. They are part of a bedroom suite of two washstands, two commodes, a cheval mirror and a bedside cabinet with drawers which belonged to the Duke of Cleveland. The Victorian washstand set is Minton.

91. 'Mulberry Chrysanthemum' decorating an 1899 Shanks 'Torrens' cistern, 'of high sanitary efficiency and beautiful appearance'. It was available in either copper lined mahogany or vitro porcelain.

92. A Twyfords paper box of the early 1900s, made to fit onto the back of the seat of the 'Twycliffe Patent Syphon WC Basin'. Paper boxes were often made to match both the pedestals and the cisterns and this ornate design 'Corinthian', in relief, was sold with a closet decorated with the most handsome frieze of royal blue and gold pillars.

90. Three bourdaloues, the conveniently shaped receptacles for ladies to slip between their legs. They were first used in France in the early eighteenth century, but by the mid eighteenth century were being made all over Europe and even in China and Japan for export. One from China still exists with the words 'Take pity gentle maid' in English. They were made at Meissen in Germany, some with mirrors on the bottom, encircled with words 'Aux plaisirs des dames', and another from Meissen in the Musée des Arts Decoratifs in Paris has the words, in Spanish 'Oh if I could see'.

The derivation of the word bourdaloue is confused: most of the puzzle centres round the figure of Père Bourdaloue, the Jesuit preacher in ordinary to Louis XIV who ladies flocked to hear and, loath to miss a minute of his brilliance, they took with them these useful containers hidden in their muffs.

These three are at Raby Castle, County Durham. The two on the left are of earthenware, made in the nineteenth century. The plainer more elegant version is of porcelain and dates from the late eighteenth century.

93. The slipper bath belonging to Sir Walter Calverley Blackett of Wallington Hall, Cambo, Northumberland.

The slipper bath (which is not in its usual position) is surrounded by a collection of objects gathered together by the National Trust which now runs the house. There is a nineteenth-century Minton washstand set with weaving pink ribbons, a woollen jug cosy, two brass and one china hot water carriers, 'Dr Nelson's Improved Inhaler' and two more, one in marble veined china, a razor strop box, a sunlight soap box, a bottle of Aperient Mineral Water by Aquaperia of Harrogate, a pewter bed pan, a china slop bucket, three pomade pots, two china bottles, a 'ring tree', a decanter and glass, a china hot water bottle, the most beautiful lace edged hand towels and a late-eighteenth-century pot cupboard. The bath is made from pieces of sheet metal, the little tap on the toe is for draining, the funnel at the front for adding hot water. Marat was knifed to death in such a bath.

94

95

94. 'The Cameo Toilet Fixture' made by the British Perforated Paper Company that was established in 1880. Part of the complete turn of the century bathroom that survives at Kinloch Castle on the Island of Rhum.

95. A perfect, complete surviving nineteenth-century water closet in Kinloch Castle on the island of Rhum with matching cistern. This is the Shanks patent 'Levern' single trap syphonic, which could only be bought in combination with the cistern to ensure that its complicated syphonic action worked perfectly. For sale in 1899, it was available in twelve different floral patterns, the one shown is 'Mulberry Chrysanthemum'.

97. Boldings 'Pillar' pedestal closet made of cast-iron enamelled with porcelain in the glittering quartz marble cloakroom designed by William de Morgan at 8 Addison Road, London, the extraordinarily elaborate house built by Halsey Ricardo for Sir Ernest Debenham of Debenham and Freebody in 1906.

96. 'Doulton's Special Closet Seat' at West Dean, near Chichester, Sussex. A handsome disguise for the lavatory pan, this specially designed chair and enclosure was available in either oiled teak, polished mahogany or walnut. 'If desired, the seat can be made to work with a seat action closet with two methods of furnishing. One so that the water continues flushing the whole time the closet is in use, and a second pattern which flushes only when the user rises from the seat.' So said the 1899 Doulton catalogue.

98

99

100

98 and 100. 'The Acme of Luxurious Bathing'. A Shanks patent 'Eureka' bath in a 'Superior Bath Cabinet' at Kinloch Castle on the island of Rhum. Usually there would only have been three taps fitted, but Lady Bullough had six, controlling the extraordinary water acrobatics: Douche, Shower, Jet, Spray, Wave, Plunge and Sitz.

99. 'Shanks Patent Independent Plunge, Spray and Shower Bath' of 1896 belonging to the Misses Besso of Withington in Manchester.

101. A hooded 'Keyhole' bath surrounded by
William De Morgan tiles at Pownall Hall, Wilmslow
in Cheshire. This delicate repeating pattern would
have been done entirely by hand.

102. The 1885 bathroom of Gledhow Hall, Leeds,
tiled throughout with Burmantoft's faience. The
marble-topped bath has sadly been taken out as has
the inside of the fireplace.

103. The washbasin in the gentleman's lavatory of the Princess
Louise Public House, High Holborn, London. Part of the 1871
remodelling of the interior by Arthur Chitty.

104. The Gothic swimming pool at Mount Stuart on the Island of
Bute, which was built in the early part of the twentieth century for
the Fourth Marquis of Bute.

104

105. Lord Bute's bathroom of
1873 at Cardiff Castle, designed
by the scholarly and eccentric
architect, William Burges for his
scholarly and eccentric patron,
the third Marquis of Bute. This
bathroom has sixty panels of
polished marble, all named, inset
into the walls of Central American
mahogany.

106. Red marble 'Roman' Bath at Port Lympne in Kent installed by Sir Phillip Sassoon, c.1920.

107. Lord Bute's roman bath at Cardiff Castle. Reputedly brought from Italy, it was inset with metal sea creatures (the plug-hole is a starfish) to designs by William Burges, for the batchelor bathroom in the Clock Tower at Cardiff.

108. The Edrios, a valve closet by John Bolding and Sons, at Castle Drogo, the enormous pile built by Lutyens near Exeter in Devon for Julius Charles Drewe between 1911–30. All the lavatories, each in a little room designed with the utmost care in granite and oak by Lutyens, were installed after the First World War.

109. Lord Curzon's bath at Montacute, the late-sixteenth-century house in Somerset that he rented from 1915 until his death in 1925. The magnificent and imperious Lord Curzon, Viceroy of India and holder of innumerable other distinguished positions, who when delivering speeches was likened by Labouchere to 'a divinity addressing black-beetles', was in constant and irksome pain from the age of nineteen until the day he died. He had curvature of the spine and was always to wear a steel corset, which very possibly was the reason for him building this conveniently private bath into his bedroom when he redecorated many of the rooms at Montacute.

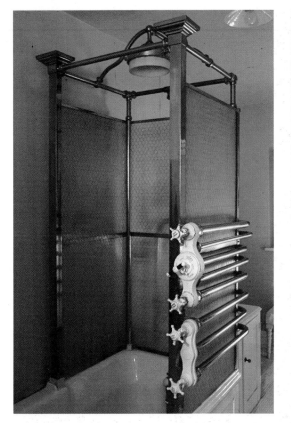

110. The salt and fresh water bath installed for Lady Astor at Sandwich Bay in Kent in 1910. Shanks provided the bath, with the 'extra inlet', an additional fitting that was manufactured by them for salt, soft or hard water supplies. The sea water was piped to the house, where it was raised by a two cylinder pump into the storage tanks. One, heated by a boiler, supplied the hot salt water, the other was cold.

111. The bulging 'Radio' Adamsez urinals in the gentleman's cloakroom of the old Derry and Toms building, Kensington High Street, London. Built by Bernard George in 1933.

112. A naked behind cast in fibreglass in 1974 by Martin Cook and Roger Stone of 8 Ringford Road, London SW18. It is fixed here to a Twyfords 'Celtic' wash-down WC, a 'flush to wall' closet.